GIRLS!
GIRLS? GIRLS.

Marjuan Canady

Sepia Works LLC
Washington, DC

Girls! Girls? Girls. Copyright ©2010 Marjuan Canady

Girls! Girls? Girls. is published by Sepia Works LLC

All rights reserved. No part of this book may be reproduced in any form or by any means, electronic or mechanical, including photocopying or recording, or by an information storage and retrieval system, without permission in writing from the publisher.

Professionals and amateurs are herby warned that this material, being fully protected under the Copyright Laws of the United States of America and all other countries of the Berne and Universal Copyright Conventions, is subject to a royalty. All rights including, but not limited to, professional, amateur, recording, motion picture, recitation, lecturing, public reading, radio and television broadcasting, and the rights of translation into foreign languages are expressly reserved. Particular emphasis is placed on the question of readings and all uses of this book by educational institutions, permissions for which must be secured from the author's representative.

Lyrics are copyright © 2010 Marjuan Canady

Cover design and formatting by Nabeeh Bilal

For my future daughters.

Girls! Girls? Girls.

Thank You

Noelle Ghoussaini

Shadae Lamar Smith

India Bolds

Ernesto Guadalupe

Carol Jagdeo

Tracy Brown

Quatis Tarkington

Randy Martin

Matthew Maguire

Tatiana Johnson

Jason Battle

Nabeeh Bilal

Jonathan McCrory

New York University, Tisch School of the Arts, Arts Politics Department

Fordham University, Theatre Department

Girls! Girls? Girls.

Production History

Girls! Girls? Girls. premiered Off-Broadway at Theatre Row at The United Solo Theatre Festival in New York, New York on November 17, 2010.

Written by Marjuan Canady

Performed by Marjuan Canady

Directed by Noelle Ghoussaini

Produced by Marjuan Canady

Music by Frank Zurita

Videography by Shadae Lamar Smith

Choreographed by India Bolds

Stage Managed by Chris Larkin

Girls! Girls? Girls.

Characters

Beverly Brushetta, a news anchor

Briana Brushetta, Beverly's 17 year old daughter

40 Ounce, a rapper from Miami, FL

Roberto Astacio, a Dominican man from the Bronx, NY

Susan "Gisela" Sosnowski, a Caucasian woman from Upper Manhattan

Saartjie "The Venus" Hottentot, a South African woman

Jessica Schnyder, a 17 year old Caucasian girl from Connecticut

Sharon Thomas, a Trinidadian secretary

Janelle "Superthroat" Vaszquez, a 17 year old Afro-Latina girl from Brooklyn, NY

Mama Jenkins, an Afro-centric, African-American woman

Place

A city, maybe New York City.

Time

The present or future.

Playwright's Note

This play was originally created for one woman to portray all ten characters. However, this play may cast multiple actresses of color to portray the characters. The setting should be spare but characters should have bold and colorful props that bring the characters to life. Satire fills every character and moment in the play. It is disgustingly and frighteningly funny, it is a heightened reality, revealing truth. Hip-Hop and pop culture are on overload. Transitions are critical to the life of this play, whether performed solo or with multiple actresses. Each character influences one another and needs each other for their own survival.

Girls! Girls? Girls.

From the Playwright

I wrote this play eight years in my apartment in New York City. I was a frustrated 23 year old actress, trying to "make it" in the Big Apple. My eyes were just opening to the injustices I faced as a woman of color in the entertainment industry and the larger society. Unable to get work and constantly labeled as "other", I decided to step out of the box and create a play on what people really think about black women, what history has said about them and what our future might look like if we continue on this path. This play features ten unique voices from the same community, who are all influenced by history and one another. This play has grown from a basement, to a black box theater, to train stations to schools, parks, community centers, to Off-Broadway, to national theaters and to the big screen.

This play has taken me around the world, got young people talking and thinking about the power of the media, the role it has in their lives and what they can do as active change agents. This play has reminded me the power of my own voice, the dedication, sacrifice and commitment needed to make art for change. It has restored my spirit as a creative artist and a woman. Thank you to my entire team over the years who made this work come alive on stage and on screen, Noelle, Shadae, Ezra, India, Quatis, Ernesto, Tatiana, Jason and my mom Carol. I dedicate this play to all the women who are making their own way and living in their light.

-Marjuan Canady

Girls! Girls? Girls.

From the Director

I am so honored to have directed Girls! Girls? Girls., a project close to my heart. Marjuan and I began collaborating on this powerful piece after finishing our Masters degree together. And here it is, eight years later: getting published, touring, a film documentary, a hilarious and pertinent play that is still highly sought after.

Marjuan's witty satire and her acute perceptions of cultural inequity and appropriation keep us laughing as well as ask us to do some deep reflection. How do the images, narratives of the media shape and define us, both consciously and subconsciously?
How do we embody, resist or appropriate identities? The ten diverse characters of this piece bring us into an imagined world in the not so distant future. The slight removal from our present reality reveals many of the absurdities of our current cultural landscape; and we see the media bubble and its impact on black and brown women world-wide with fresh eyes. I love this play and believe in the power of each of its character's stories, I know you will too.

-Noelle Ghoussaini

Girls! Girls? Girls.

Introduction

This play takes place in the future. Sometime close but yet far away in the distance. Maybe 2050. Maybe not. Maybe New York City. Maybe Not. The characters are as real as one can imagine them. They are all searching for something bigger, bigger then what they know. The characters do not particularly know each other but exist in similar spaces.

Lights up on Beverly Brushetta's daughter, Briana Brushetta. She is secretly getting dressed for the 40 Ounce "Pussy Rims" audition. She sees herself in the mirror and loves and hates herself. Her beauty confuses her. She turns on music. We hear an empowering woman's song. She turns on the television. She sees her mother on the Beverly Brushetta Talk Show. She ignores her.

Beverly Brushetta is seen in the audience as she talks to the imaginary camera. She holds a microphone.

GIRLS!
GIRLS? GIRLS.

Girls! Girls? Girls.

BEV TALK

Beverly Brushetta is the host and front woman of the Black Women's Network. She is a conformist and assimilationist. She moves with robotic movement. Strong eyes, big smile, Uncle Tom-like. She wears obnoxious glasses.

Beverly Brushetta:
Hello there and welcome to Bev Talk on The Black Woman's Network, where everyday, it's a Black Woman's Thang. I'm Beverly Brushetta, the most powerful woman in the media. Is this audience ready for what we have in store today? Great. I love your enthusiasm! Let's get started!

Progressive platinum rap artist and activist 40 Ounce, is on the hunt to find his lucky leading lady to star in his new music video, Pussy Rims, and he has asked all of us here at Bev Talk to help him in his search. But he needs your help America! Today, you will vote for the qualities you want to see in the next Pussy Rim Chick.

Now, the qualities that are most important to 40 and his team are race, hair, skin, eye color, buttocks and breast size. By the end of the program, using our state of the art BWN satellite system, we will announce who will be the next Pussy Rim Chick! Now, lets get to the man himself, critically acclaimed hip hop pioneer, 40 Ounce has given Bev Talk backstage access into his recording studio where he is laying down the remix to his hit song Pussy Rims. 40, where you at brother?

Girls! Girls? Girls.

Girls! Girls? Girls.

THE STUDIO

40 Ounce is seen. He is a southern rapper who dreams of everything money. He is a good guy, just lost, plays into the stereotype. He is boisterous and direct but he is focused in the studio. He has skills. He hides his true self. He is inebriated. He performs well for the camera.

40 Ounce:

What's up America? How ya doin Bev? It's ya boy 40, comin' straight from the studio. Right now, we in here with my girl Thug Misses, laying down the remix to Pussy Rims. This song, it's about goin out, having a good time, na mean, wit the ladies… so ladies, if you think you that next Pussy Rim Chick, I betta see you at the audition, aight. Right now, we about to give you a sneak peek of the remix.

He talks to the sound engineer, PeeWee.

Where my headphones at? Aight. Where my drink at? Aight.

He picks up his 40 juice and takes a gulp.
He looks back to the camera.

America, this that 40 juice. Gutta Money bringing the realest juice to ya lips right now. Aight, Peewee...drop the beat.

He begins to rap.

Girls! Girls? Girls.

Uhh..Uhh..Damn baby got her hair down her back wit an ass so phat and a waist like a Tic Tac. That's how I like my hoes, they drop it real low bounce that ass like a yo-yo.
I don't know how she get, Baartman Bottom Jeans on,
wit a thong on. Stank panties up her crack, rat tat, tat,
like that, from the back, c'mon. I get Pussy and Rims Bitch...I get Pussy and Rims Bitch...I get...

A voice over of the sound engineer interrupts him. He is very proper.

Voice Over:

Hold up, Hold up 40! Lets take the chorus back, you were a little flat on the second pussy. Let's take it again.

40 Ounce:

Aight...That's what i'm talking about Pee-Wee. C'mon. Drop the beat.

The Pussy Rims beat is heard.

Girls! Girls? Girls.

THE D EXPRESS

We see Roberto Astacio, a Dominican man about 30-something years old. He is from the Bronx, NY. He wears big headphones on a New York, D subway car listening and rapping to 40 Ounce's song Pussy Rims. He exists in his own world with little regard for those around him. He is an intellectual and well versed in black feminist scholarship but his misogyny overpowers him. He sings loudly. He notices a young woman staring at him. He has a heavy Dominican accent.

Roberto:
What? Wassup? What you looking at? Mami, I see you looking at me!? I ain't do nuthin'. I ain't wildin' out like that homeless man over there. Aaah. See, I got you to smile mami! He laughs. Mira, I apologize if I'm disturbing you but this new Gutta Money track by 40 Ounce, Pussy Rims just dropped. This shit is fire ma!

The video gonna drop soon, it gon be number 1, guarantee you that, straight from the Bronx. Mira, mami, ¿te gusta lo que ves? Mami te ves bellizima.

Oh lo siento, my bad, you don't speak Spanish. You mad beautiful, dead ass, looking all intellectual and shit... reading "Still Brave: The Evolution of Black Women's Studies" with your sexy Assata Shakur pin. Mami, have you ever read Bell Hook's "Ain't I A Woman?" The dopest chapter is on slave life and black women. I totally agree with Hooks when she suggests that black women suffered more than the so called emasculated black man. They had to be both woman and man at the same time!!

He laughs hysterically.

Mira! Ahhhhhh, see! You didn't think I knew that shit! ...So let me get your number.

Oh! My music? You gotta problem wit that Gutta Money? Look ma, I been around sistas like you before but I'm sensing that you ain't really feelin my presence on this train right now. Hello? Mami! I'm talking to you!

He turns to the passenger sitting next to him on the train.

See that's what's wrong wit sistas like her. Cuz they go to school and read these books that say rap is sexist and shit. I know about misogyny and essentializing identities. I know your language. Rap ain't make that shit up B. That shit was there before hip-hop. Because they real bitches and hoes out here willin' to do whatever it takes to get they paper.

I just walked by the convention center and seen a line full of hoes lined up trying to be 40 Ounce's newest Pussy Rim Chick. I would never let my daughter do that shit but if those hoes willin' to line themselves up, I'm willing to look at the line, you know. Don't be mad at me, be mad at them. I'm just listening to this shit.

He mumbles.

Como Mierda.

Girls! Girls? Girls.

He becomes enraged, stands up and moves to the center of the car train.

EXCUSE ME, LADIES AND GENTLEMAN!
I HAVE AN ANNOUNCEMENT TO MAKE! MY NAME IS ROBERTO
AND I'M FROM THE BRONX AND I NEED EVERYBODY HERE TO KNOW,
I AM NOT A SEXIST! I MAY BE LISTENING TO 40 OUNCE'S PUSSY
RIMS BUT I AM NOT A SEXIST. I AM SIMPLY REACTING TO THIS OP-
PRESSIVE SYSTEM THAT WOMEN HAVE PLACED ON ME.
WE CAN'T FUNCTION PROPERLY AS MEN UNTIL WOMEN
CHOOSE TO ACT RIGHT.

He moves in closer to the young woman.
I hope you heard what I said ma cuz you not gonna find the answer in that little book you reading. ¿Quien te crei? ¡Tu no eres nada! ¡Come mierda!

He puts his headphones back on,
mumbling some Spanish under his breath.
The train doors open. A young woman walks on the train.
She is wearing Baartman Bottom jeans.

Damn!!!!

He stares at her ass.
He speaks to her.

Girls! Girls? Girls.

Oye chica....Sweetie! Can I conversate for a minute with u ma? Mami....I was just admiring… your smile.

He is staring at her bottom.

What's your name? Briana.
That's mad sexy. Where are you going looking all sexy? Samba class!? Damn, I could tell as soon as I seen you that you was mad cultured. See a girl like you, needs to be with a man like me. You feel me? So what's up? Lemme get your mathematics.

Girls! Girls? Girls.

SEXUALLY FREE

Susan "Gisela" Sosnowski is a samba enthusiast and over zealous white woman. She is about 45. She is not a good samba dancer.

Susan "Gisela" Sosnowski:
Great class everyone! Ashe! Ashe!

A beginner student approaches her.

Great class, right. Is this your first class? Oh, what's your name? Briana Bru-she-tta... daughter of Beverly Brushetta?! Oh my goodness!! Please tell your mom, I'm one of her biggest fans! I watch her everyday and I absolutely love these BWN samba classes! They are a little pricey but it's no biggie for me because it really allows people like me to get in touch with world culture! So what brings you to class? Oh really? You are auditioning for a hip hop video? Wow, good for you girlfriend! Well this class will definitely allow you to tap into your inner sexuality.

She chuckles to herself.

It's a little strange at first but you really have to release into the drums and the gods in the room. The orishas are here with us. Yes! All of them, as we speak, there's Ogun, Yemoja, Chango. I really root myself into the ground and allow Chango to enter my spirit.

She is interrupted by the other women leaving class.

Tchau! Tchau! See you girls next week!! Mantenha cuadril aberto! Keep those hips loose and open!

She refocuses back to Briana.

Girls! Girls? Girls.

Oh, no! I'm not from Brasil. But I have visited many times.
I plan to relocate there in a couple of years.
The way of living, the people, the freeing atmosphere,
it's so inviting.

You know Brasil is one of the few countries in the world
that is race free. I mean, I think this is why it's paradise,
because everyone is excepted, equal and considered equal.
The most beautiful women in the world are from there, like
the Globeleza. Have you ever heard of her?
They use this woman to promote carnival in Brazil
six months before it begins.

The Globeleza is everything every woman wants to be, her body
is flawless, she has the perfect tan and the absolute most
beautiful hair. She's like Beyonce. We all want to be like B
right?

The Globeleza is Brazil's Beyonce! Yes! This is a real woman!
Her commercial airs in Brazil every two to three minutes for
months and get this, she's completely naked.
Now that's power. That's why I'm here taking samba class
because I want to be the next Globeleza! I know, I don't
exactly look like her but I figure I can get all of that
fixed when I get to Rio. I just have to tan,
get some implants here and there and Samba my way to the top.

Even though I am just learning Samba, I do have the most important element down pact, I am sexually free.

Girls! Girls? Girls.

See that's the difference between American and Brazilian women, especially those mulattas. They love to be naked. They're practically born that way.

I hope this new denim line, Baartman Bottoms, that's coming out will allow American women to find their own sexual freedom. American woman are pretty desperate. So… how about yourself? Are you sexually free?

I saw you struggling a bit with some of the more basic steps. Look! If I give you a little bit of advice, I guarantee you, you'll get that part at that audition! Trust me, I know what I'm talking about. I got my Ph.D. in Afro-Brazilian Religious Performance Memory from Yale. Ok, try this with me.

She begins to demonstrate the movement.

You want to root yourself into the ground and allow Chango to enter your spirit, allow him to release in your pelvis.

She begins to gyrate her pelvis back and forth.
She goes faster and faster and faster.
She is uncoordinated.

And Release! And Release! Release! Release! Release! Release! Release! Release! GIRLFRIEND! You are a professional! You're gonna walk into those auditions and show them who's in charge! And you'll get that part! Good Luck!

She begins to exit.

Girls! Girls? Girls.

Oh, desculpe. I didn't even tell you my name,

I'm Susan but you can call me Gisela.

Girls! Girls? Girls.

BWN ICON OF THE MONTH

The Black Women's Network theme song is heard.

Beverly Brushetta:

Good afternoon. Beverly Brushetta, here. Here at BWN, we believe in today, yesterday and tomorrow. That's why we celebrate great black women in our history.

This month's BWN icon is none other then, Sara Saartije Baartman, The Venus, The Venus Hottentot. No matter what you call her. She is a woman of magnificent dimensions. Let's take a look.

We see an educational video on the Venus Hottentot.

Marjuan Canady as "Beverly Brushetta"

Girls! Girls? Girls. documentary, 2013. Photo courtesy of Sepia Works.

Canady as "Saartjie Baartman"

University of New Haven, 2012. Photo courtesy of Sepia Works.

Girls! Girls? Girls.

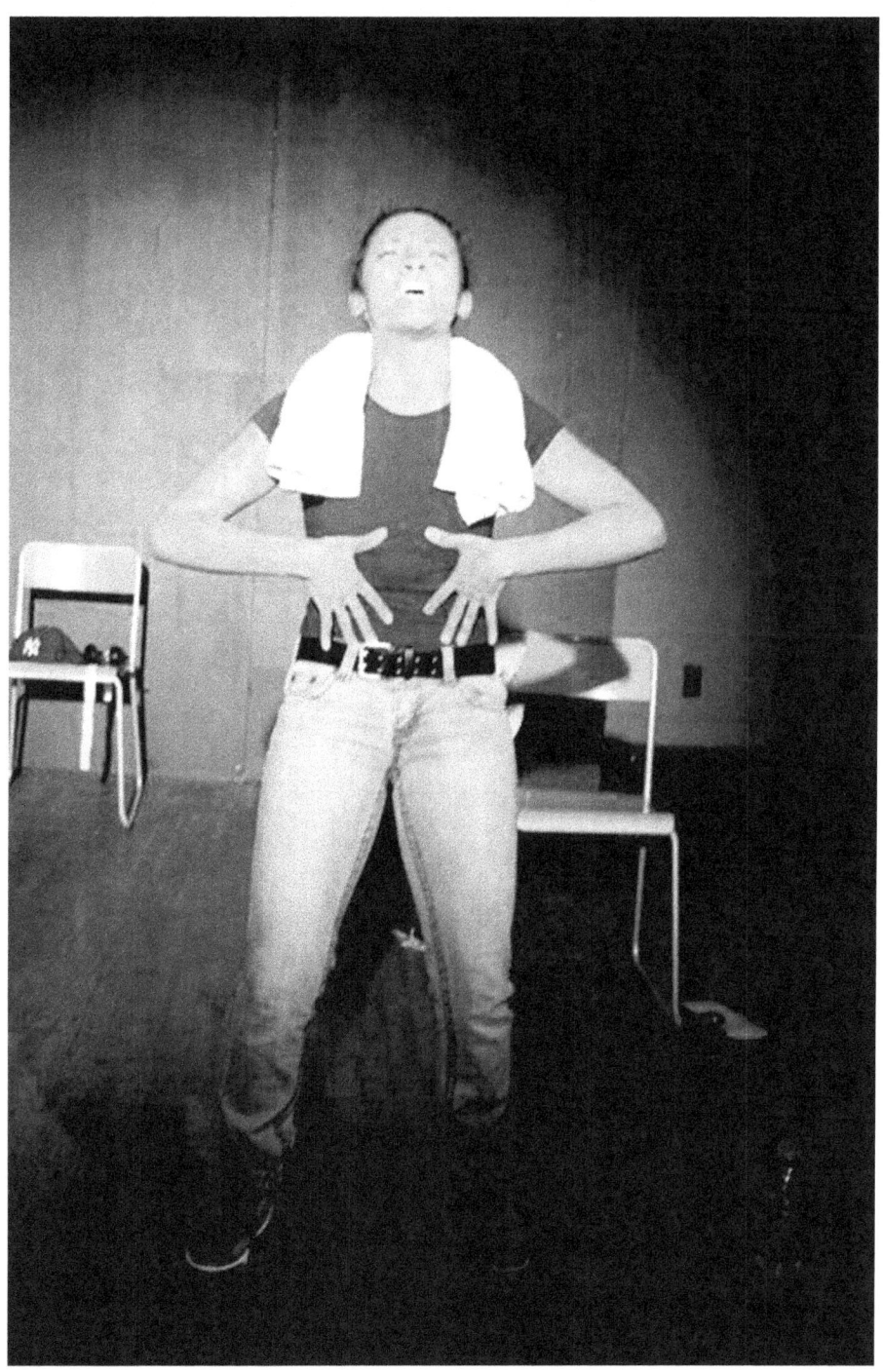

Off-Broadway, 2010. Photo courtesy of Sepia Works.

Tiffin University, 2012. Photo courtesy of Sepia Works.

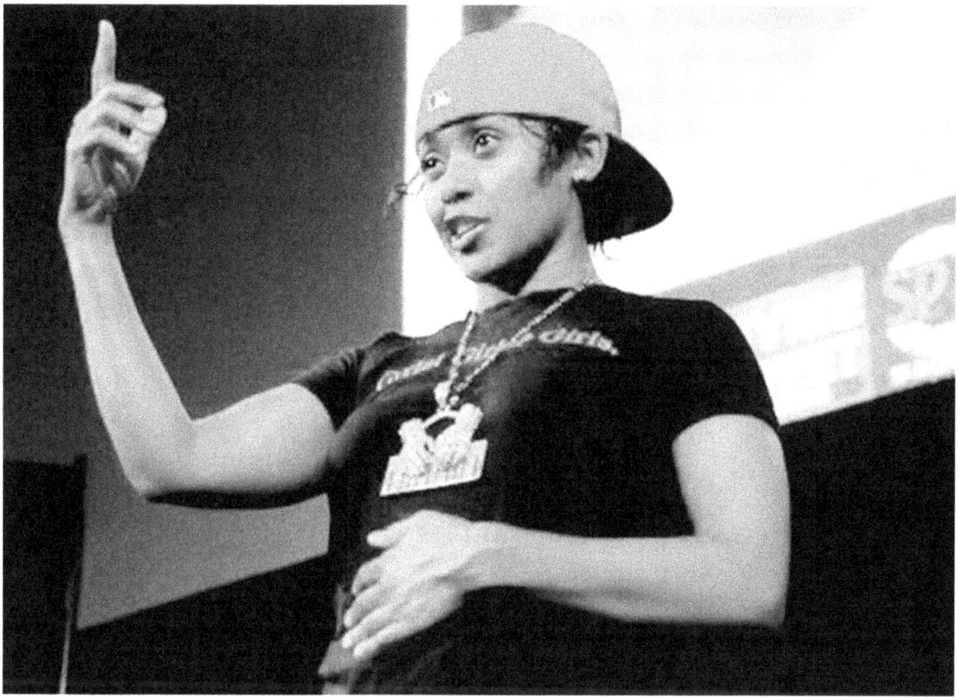

Girls! Girls? Girls.

Canady as "40 Ounce"

Love Us Festival, 2012. Photo courtesy of Love Us Festival.

Canady as "Roberto Astacio"

George Washington University, 2011. Photo courtesy of Sepia Works.

Girls! Girls? Girls.

Girls! Girls? Girls.

BAARTMAN BOTTOMS

A misogynistic hip-hop booty song is heard. The space is transformed into a museum. Lights up on the 21st century Sara The Venus Hottentot Baartman. She stands frozen elevated behind a glass window. She wears her Baartman Bottom jeans and fabulous sun glasses.

Spectators walk back and forth observing her. She comes to life watching them as they pass.

Saartjie "Venus" Baartman:
Psss. Psss. Psss. Hey! Hey you! Miss! I'm talking to you.

It's me, it's ya girl Saartjie. Sara. The Venus, Saartije, Sara Baartman, The Venus Hottentot! Don't act like you don't know me especially after all the bullshit I've been through.

I'm sorry, I usually don't get that many visitors, not since they put me down here in the primitive peoples of ancient civilization section. Have you come here to get advice for these 40 Ounce auditions? Look, girl, you not the only one who needs my expertise. I'll tell you, like I told the one before, it's all in the bottoms baby. If you know how to work that ass, you'll get the part. But the only way to work that ass, is if you have a pair of my new line of jeans, Baartman Bottoms.

Now two things that make Baartman Bottoms absolutely fabulous:

One, easily accessible. You can find us in your living room on your television set on BWN, BET, MTV, VH1, TVONE, Centric and

of course your local departments stores
and limited boutiques.

Two, our denim technology is so
advanced. We customize your denim to shape your bottom.
So, each Baartman Bottom is a one of kind original.
Fabulous right!? You will love the feeling knowing that your
ass is on the spotlight. Trust me, I know.

> *The museum manager walks by.*

Shhh. Here's come the museum manager!

> *She quickly adjusts herself back to her beginning statue position. He exits. She takes a deep breath.*

He's gone. I hate the people in here. The museum world has maintained my image for the past 233 years and now they just hatin' on me because people finally realizing I'm the true inventor of the black female ass and the public still wants me. I'm the truth!

My favorite moment of the public is when their eyes bulge out of their head as if they've never seen anything like me before. Honey! I am a star!

> *She laughs hysterically and uncontrollably.*
> *Briana begins to walk away.*

Girls! Girls? Girls.

Wait! Wait! Please, please don't go! Don't leave me! Please!

What's your name? Briana. Oh that's nice. I have to confess, ever since I partnered with 40 Ounce and his 40 Juice, I've become an alcoholic and I throw my food up from time to time but I'm just trying to keep my waist tight. Damn it! It's hard out here for an ass! I'm just trying to make some cash.

If all these corporations and rappers can make millions off my ass, don't you think I should be able to profit in it too? Right? Right?! Right?!

She takes a breath and collects herself.

Right. Baartman Bottoms will be sold everywhere, for women, plus size and petite, men who become women at night, a special line and fit for lesbians, white girls and of course baby Baartman Bottoms for little girls and infants. We gotta get them young.

You can pay for your jeans as you exit out.

She notices the museum manager coming.

Oh, it's him again!

She goes back to her original statue position.

Girls! Girls? Girls.

If you want more information about Baartman Bottoms you can visit us online at www.baartmanbottoms.com.

Girls! Girls? Girls.

THE BWN NEWS ROOM

The Black Women's Network theme song is heard.

Beverly Brushetta sits at her news desk.

Beverly Brushetta:

Good Afternoon and Welcome to the BWN Newsroom. This is Beverly Brushetta, reporting on the most critical issues facing black women today, in politics and entertainment and everything else in between.

She angles her head to camera 1.

Genital Herpes on the move. What could be facilitating HIV amongst black women could be genital herpes. The CDC recently released statistics indicating one out of six Americans have genital herpes while the infection rate of Black women is 17%. Ladies, tell him to pull out.

She angles her head to camera 2.

Moving on to national news, rapper and actress Thug Misses, the first lady of Gutta Money Records, recently had her phone stolen at a nightclub. Whoever the culprit was, uploaded embarrassing pictures of Miami's finest pair of jugs to the internet.

She is suddenly interrupted by the breaking news in her earpiece. She grabs her earpiece.

I'm sorry. Excuse me…. Wow! ...People, this just in, NFL Superstar, Crab Cinco Seis has just announced he will be

Girls! Girls? Girls.

starring in his new dating reality show, Bunting in My Pants.

To all those ladies interested in the Bunting in My Pants casting, visit Crab on his Baller's alert page, upload your sexiest pic and use the hashtag, #buntinmypants.

She angles her head to camera 3.

Finally onto community news, rap artist and activist, 40 Ounce will hold his auditions for his new music video Pussy Rims in fifteen minutes. We here at BWN are proud to be sponsors of this historic audition, where one lucky lady will not only be the featured in Pussy Rims but will also grace the cover of Pussy Swagger Magazine and receive a whopping $500 cash.

Ladies, it's time to squeeze into your Baartman Bottoms and head to the auditions today. Stay here with BWN, for more breaking news by the hour.

This is Beverly Brushetta. It's a black woman's thang.

Girls! Girls? Girls.

YOUTUBE

A popular pop song is heard.

Bedroom. Jessica, a 17-year-old Caucasian girl, is setting up her video camera and adjusting it.

She is preparing to premiere her newest booty twirk dance video to her online fans.

She is wearing Baartman Bottom jeans. She is a bad dancer.

Jessica:

Like, good afternoon Youtube and America this is Jessica Schnyder from New Haven, Connecticut, Church and Chapel! And I am so happy to be here with all of my fans. Today is so important because I am beginning my career. Today, I am auditioning for 40 Ounce's new video Pussy Rims and I will be the principal girl, just look at me, I'm HOT! America, check out my new Baartman Bottoms. My ass looks awesome, right? But my secret today, won't be in my bottoms like the rest of those girls, it will be in these bad girls.

She grabs her breast.

I can guarantee you no one in the audition room will have these. 40 Ounce could totally have my soy latte ass! Anyway, as many of you know, working in this industry can be so frustrating and discriminatory. I swear it's like, sexist, reverse racism against white girls who want to break into the hip-hop entertainment industry. I'm going to prove today youtube, that I am the hottest white girl… I mean hottest girl and snag the principle role.

Girls! Girls? Girls.

She is interrupted by her mother.

She yells down the hallway.

Yes, mom I'm almost ready! All my lacrosse stuff is downstairs. I'll be down in a sec. I'm just packing my books up.

She focuses back to the camera.

Sorry America. You know how parents can get. But I wanted to give you a sneak peak of how I'm going lay it down in the audition room. Feel free to leave your comments below. I want to give a shout out to my boy 40 Ounce for always keeping it real, by making real music for big booty hoes.

She turns on 40 Ounce's Pussy Rims and begins booty dancing.

She seduces the camera and then begins to dance faster. She has little rhythm and is more concerned about looking like a video model in the camera then dancing. Her mom's voice suddenly interrupts her. She turns her music off and sticks her head out the bedroom door.

What Mom?!!! They're in the closet. If Uncle Dave's golf clubs aren't there, then I don't know where they are. What? I'm play this music to pump me up for practice. I'll be down in a second. Don't be a hater, yo!

She turns back to the camera.

Girls! Girls? Girls.

Sorry. I'm not going to lacrosse practice. My best friend Briana and I are going to skip our lacrosse practice and take the Metro North to the auditions. We're total bad assess. Well, I hope you enjoyed what you saw because the next time you see me, I'll be glossed up on the beach getting pizzaid with my girl B and my boy 40.

Her mom interrupts her again. She is upset.

LOOK MOM, I SAID DON'T INTERRUPT ME WHEN I'M FOCUSING ...What? She's here? Oh, My gosh! Briana is here!

She yells down the hallway.
Hey Briana! What it is hoe?
I'll be down in a second girlfriend!

She focuses back to the camera.
Ok, America, I have to go but don't forget to inbox me your comments. I'm a little nervous but I know I got this. Wish me luck. A star is in the making.

Peace up, Losers Down.

Girls! Girls? Girls.

Girls! Girls? Girls.

CARNIVAL

Reception area of law firm Leman, Smith and Mire. Sharon Thomas, a 40 something year old Trinidadian secretary leisurely reads a Caribbean magazine. She wears a headset and is doing everything but working. When she speaks on the phone, she tries her best to disguise her heavy Caribbean accent.

Sharon Thomas:

> *The telephone rings. She hides her accent on the phone.*

Lehman, Smith and Mire, can you hold please?

> *She continues to look through her magazine.*

Why it seem everyone call me when I need a smoke? It a damn conspiracy.

> *The telephone rings. She picks up.*
> *She hides her accent.*

Lehman, Smith and Mire, can you hold please?

Vinny, I need a smoke break in five! Yes, I still have to leave early today. I have to pick my niece Briana up from the convention center. She's auditioning for some 40 Ounce music video. You know how these chil'ren take up wit dem yankee rappers and tings.

These chil'ren have no idea that hip hop would be nothing if it weren't for Caribbeans coming to the Bronx. We, Trini's never get credit for anything we do. Vinny... You listening to me? Hello!? Well, I leavin' early tomorrow too.

Girls! Girls? Girls.

Yes, boy, I get a real cheap flight, wit that new airline, British Commonwealth Wings.

Yes boy! I goin' to jump up in Miami carnival. See, you know nothing about mas, nothing about freein up yaself. For ten years, I dedicating to the practice of freeing up me self, every year, ya hear me, every year!

The Pussy Rim auditions appear on tv.
Oh shit! Look the auditions are on! Turn it up!

A video is seen of women auditioning for 40 Ounce's Pussy Rims music video. Sharon is disgusted.
I tell you, these young girls are something else. They just so damn fast, ready to expose they saltfish for anyone just for a buck. I hope Briana tellin' her mother, she participating in some filthy, filthy sex show cuz I ain't takin' no part in it. But we all know how her mother, done changed. Ya see Vinny, I used to play mas with my sister, but now she actin' all biggish because she got some high profile job. I have a high profile job here too but when it time to play mas, I let it hang loose. Vinny, you come and play mas with me one time and feel what it like to free up ya self, act dotish, drink rum, wine up the place, eat as much curry goat, roti and callaloo, as you want.

What?! You see you, you, Americans have nothing in your culture that shows ya pride! That why ya stink.

Girls! Girls? Girls.

That why any chance ya get ya run down to da islands to find peace and tranquility. But we Caribbeans have peace and tranquility everyday!

>*The telephone rings. She speaks into the phone.*
>*She hides her accent.*

Lehman, Smith and Mire. Can you hold...

>*The person on the phone cuts her off.*
>*She does not hide her accent anymore.*

Well I put you on hold because someone is ahead of your call! Now hold please!

She hangs the phone up.

So damn rude. Where was I? Oh yes, peace and tranquility... You see, I plan my entire year around carnival, Miami, Eastern Parkway in Brooklyn, DC and Caribana, Toronto. I go, because they each have a different flava. But you know what is the ultimate Carnival? Trinidadian carnival. Because a Trini really know how to party! We throw baccannal like no other. For months people partying, stop work and drink Old Oak, Rum and Punch, wit a cold Stag or Carib. I mostly play in the mud band tho, because it a cheap, cheap way to free up yourself and you only need ya bra and panty to wine to soca and chutney.

She begins to sing a soca song loudly.

What you mean, you don't see the point of Carnival?

Girls! Girls? Girls.

I tell you what the point is, to free up yourself and let it hang loose. Why we celebrate it? Because...because it our history. It in our blood. Look you asking to many damn questions. Why you acting like a chupide? I just a woman that play mas, drink Carib and throw mud at people.
You know, you's a real maco-man, I know where Carnival come from...

Vinny leaves the room.

Vinny! Vinny! Vinny! Come back!

The telephone rings.
She answers in her Caribbean Accent.

Lehman, Smith and Mire. WE CLOSED!!

She looks around, making sure Vinny is gone.
She types into her computer and painfully stares at the screen.

...The History of Caribbean Carnival.

THE GUEST

The Black Women's Network theme song is heard.

Beverly Brushetta:

Welcome back to Bev Talk. Have you ever wondered what it's like to be a real hoe? Please help me welcome today's Bev Talk special guest to the studio, Janelle Vasquez, aka, Superthroat, a sixteen year old hoe from Brooklyn, NY whom specializes her line of work in the Bronx. She has been working in this profession since the age of thirteen. Wow! What a professional!

Ladies and gentlemen, Superthroat!

Girls! Girls? Girls.

Girls! Girls? Girls.

REAL LOVE

Janelle "Superthroat" Vasquez is a 16-year-old Afro-Latina young woman from Brooklyn who works as a prostitute in the Bronx. She is a fast talker. She has a fake designer bag. She is excited to be on the Beverly Brushetta show.

Janelle "Superthroat" Vasquez:
Hello Beverly, studio audience, I'm really excited to be here on your show to talk about my new book and all my new work I got goin' on.

How did I get into this business? Well it seems so long ago, but I think I started when I was thirteen, when my parents split. I'm sixteen now. I just didn't want to be in the house so a good friend of mine, Sean, he's my pimp now, he got me started, but back then, we was just friends.
He was older then me, and he always had mad nice stuff and I wanted to have nice stuff too, you know.

Bev, you should have seen him, he pulled up in this fly car, it must have been a maserati or aston martin or somethin'. He told me how I had a nice thang going on. They always try to be smooth and shit with you in the beginning. So I just kept seeing him around the way, so I let him take me to the movies, to a diner and he even took me to the Botanical Gardens. You know the one in the Bronx! No one has ever taken me there. We were in love Bev. And ladies, sometimes when you in love, you gotta sacrifice for your man.

Girls! Girls? Girls.

Like in the beginning, money was low, so I decided to help him out at Hunts Point… No Bev, I know how to work the block! I been there for three years and never been stopped by the police. You really just gotta make friends with them. You know what I mean? How you think I got my nickname? How much money I make? Bev, you know I'm only telling you this because you my girl… Ok.

So, on a good night, I could make $500 to $600. A slow night, sometimes $50-$100. But ladies, you never want to have a slow night because your pimp will get in your ass. Like one time, I ain't make enough in a night and Sean had to let me know, that ain't acceptable. You know, this is a business and if money ain't made, somebody gotta pay. Usually it's the hoe that gotta pay, but it's a small price to pay.

But I would never sacrifice what I been through for what I have now, you know I got mad nice things, my own brand, like my new book that just dropped, "Confessions of a Super-throat" and my new lip gloss line, "Slick Lips", for you and your Barbie.

Voiceover: SLUT!

> *Janelle turns to the audience and addresses the audience member that insulted her. Her hoodness comes out.*

Girls! Girls? Girls.

Who you calling a slut yo?! Look at you, you ain't nothing!
Look at your shoes! Look at that wack ass outfit!
You's a bum yo! Come on stage and say that shit to my face!

Suddenly Janelle catches herself and her temper.
She returns back to her seat.

I'm sorry Beverly. My therapist told me about my temper.
As I was saying, I'm all about the community and giving back
to the ladies. This is a tough business and to all those
ladies who want to break into it, you have to be focused on
your goals and what you want.

I know I'm not gonna be tricking forever.
I'm just using this as a stepping stone to move on to bigger
and better things. Ladies, when your money right, you right.
Yea, of course, there are bad things that can happen, it's
the streets, you know, but bad things happen anywhere.

I remember, one night I was smoking with Sean and some of his
friends and I woke up in this car. I kinda remember the night
but not really. I just remember a lot of guys. I went to the
police the next day but they said I couldn't press charges
because I couldn't identify anyone. That's my fault. I just
take it as a lesson learned.

What do I do in my free time? I chill mostly with my bestie
Briana… B, I mean, she's my girl you know. We just get each
other and when you got someone like that, you gotta hold on
to that or whateva.

Girls! Girls? Girls.

She becomes vulnerable.

Sean gets jealous when we hang out because we spend so much time together. It's because we close. B, tells me all the time I don't need to do what I'm doing because of what people may say about me but the truth is I don't care if people call me a bitch, a slut or a hoe, as long as I'm making paper I'm straight.

I got money, men and real love. What else do I need?

NZINGA AWARD

Beverly Brushetta:

Wow! She does have a point. What a story. Ladies and Gentlemen one more time for Superthroat!

Here at BWN we believe in our history and the advancement of the modern day global black woman and as our program comes to a close today, we would like to honor this year's most accomplished black woman with the BWN Nzinga Humanitarian Award.

This award recognizes the strength, resilience and courage of black women worldwide. The BWN board has voted and this year's Super Strong Black Woman Nzinga Award goes to…

CEO and Founder of the Save a Black Girl Foundation, Mama Jenkins!

Girls! Girls? Girls.

Girls! Girls? Girls.

SUPER STRONG BLACK WOMAN OF THE YEAR AWARD

We see Mama Jenkins, an African-American woman draped in African kente cloth and ethnic regalia and jewelry. She smokes a cigarette.

Mama Jenkins:

That's a wrap people! Thank you! Thank You! Thank you for this award tonight! Unfortunately, I'm not able to be there as I'm in sunny Los Angeles filming, Save a Black Girl, the movie. But I'd like to thank BWN for choosing me to represent the strongest black woman of the year.

I'd like to thank my sorority sisters for teaching me about community.

She performs her secret sorority hand gesture.

Especially for all those step shows in college that really laid the foundation of sisterhood. It often gets difficult maintaining my strength and being a professional, single, educated black woman but I've learned to put all of my energy into my work.

But my strength would be nothing if it wasn't for my father who ran out on my mama and me. From a young girl, I developed my unique black girl attitude and developed my ability to be a sacrificial lamb because of my father. Thank you dad. That's why, we here at The Save A Black Girl Foundation encourage fathers to leave their families by the time their daughter turns age seven. That way your daughter knows you, yearns for you and hates you all at the same time. That way your daughter can develop the strength I developed from an early age.

Thank you for continuing to support the Save a Black Girl Foundation. Touch one black girl today and she will touch you tomorrow.

Thank you BEVERLY! You look stunning!

Girls! Girls? Girls.

AND THE PUSSY CHICK IS...

Beverly Brushetta:

Bravo! Bravo! This is history in the making America. And now for the moment we have all been waiting for! We will announce right here on live television who America wants as their next Pussy Rim Chick! Let's fire up our BWN satellite system and get those votes! HIT IT!

Music is heard. Beverly dances. She is off-beat.

And the results are in... Based on the qualities you have chosen and the young ladies that auditioned today, 40 Ounce's newest Pussy Rim Chick is...

...Briana Brushetta...

She begins to laugh.
Her laughter turns from a light confused laugh
to hysterical outrage.

No, No, No! BRIANA! YOU SNUCK OUT TO THOSE AUDITIONS AFTER I TOLD YOU NO!

YOUNG LADY IF YOU ARE WATCHING THIS YOU ARE GROUNDED FOR ONE MONTH. THERE IS NO WAY YOU WILL BE ON T.V. SHAKING YOUR HINE PARTS FOR MONEY LIKE YOU ARE SOME $2 HOOKER AT HUNTS POINT! FOR THESE IGNORANT RAPPER FOOLS. DON'T YOU HAVE ANY RESPECT FOR YOURSELF!

Girls! Girls? Girls.

DIDN'T I RAISE YOU BETTER THEN THIS?

I MEAN, WHAT ARE YOU TRYING TO DO TO ME?

ARE YOU TRYING TO DESTROY ME AND MY IMAGE????!

She begins to look around, noticing that the cameras are still rolling. She is terrified.

Her voice fumbles.

Cut the cameras. It's Over.

End of play.

www.ingramcontent.com/pod-product-compliance
Lightning Source LLC
Chambersburg PA
CBHW051958290426
44110CB00015B/2291